FLAN COLLE~~GE SURVIVAL~~
COOKBOOK

Second Edition

By Tim Murphy

For information on Flannel John's Cookbooks for Guys, upcoming releases and merchandise visit www.flanneljohn.com

FLANNEL JOHN'S COLLEGE SURVIVAL COOKBOOK

TABLE OF CONTENTS

WHY A COOKBOOK FOR COLLEGE STUDENTS

I started college at Western Michigan University in Kalamazoo in 1980. As a freshman my culinary repertoire consisted of popcorn, toast and hot dogs. That was all well and good when I was living in the dorms and our cafeteria was open 12 hours a day. Reality hit during summer sessions, holiday breaks and when I moved off-campus. Sure, I had built up a great relationship with the campus pizza establishments but man cannot live on a Domino's 12-inch cheese or Bilbo's deep dish pizza alone. Since I was on a very limited budget, I couldn't always scrape up the bucks to buy one. That's why I wrote this book. I've taken some recipes from my previous books and combined them with new ones to give college students a variety of meals they can make that will taste good and save money. I remember scrounging up empty cans and bottles so I could afford a loaf of bread and a half-pound of bologna. Fortunately in Michigan, empties carried a 10-cent deposit. My best advice - learn how to cook and plan a menu. You will eat better for less money and perhaps, unlike me, you won't spend 24-years paying off those student loans.

Tim Murphy – Author

BREAKFAST

AFTER PARTY PANCAKES

12 eggs
2 cups of flour
2 cups of milk
3 tablespoons of butter
Cinnamon
Sugar

In an oven, melt butter in a 9-inch by 13-inch pan. Mix eggs, milk and flour thoroughly in a bowl and pour over butter. Don't stir. Sprinkle cinnamon and sugar on top. Bake at 425 degrees for 15 to 20 minutes.

BACON & EGGS BREAKFAST PIE

10 strips of bacon
6 eggs
3 tablespoons of milk
½ teaspoon of salt
Dash of pepper

Arrange 10 slices of cooked (but not crisp) bacon to cover the bottom and sides of an 8-inch pie plate. Beat together eggs, milk, salt and pepper. Pour mixture in the pie plate and bake at 375 degrees for 30 minutes.

BREAKAST HASH

2 cups of cooked ham or bacon, chopped
2 cups of chopped cooked potatoes
1½ onions, minced
2 tablespoons parsley
1 cup of milk
Salt and pepper
Oil

Mix all ingredients except milk. Place oil in a skillet over medium heat. When hot, spread hash mix evenly in skillet. Brown bottom of hash quickly, 10 to 15 minutes. Add milk and mix. Cover cook slowly until crisp, about 10 minutes.

BREAKFAST SAUSAGE BURGER

1 pork sausage patty
1 egg
2 bacon strips
1 slice of cheddar cheese
1 hamburger bun or English muffin

Fry sausage, egg and bacon strips in a skillet. Layer sausage, egg, bacon and cheese on a toasted bun.

CHOCOLATE CHIP PANCAKES

2 cups of Bisquick
1 cup of milk
2 eggs
½ cup of chocolate chips

Combine Bisquick, milk eggs and chocolate chips and mix well. Pour onto hot griddle and top with syrup…or chocolate sauce. This recipe also works with vanilla and butterscotch chips.

CINNAMON MONKEY BREAD

3 cans of refrigerated biscuits, quartered
1 cup of sugar
¾ cup butter
2 teaspoons cinnamon

Cook sugar, butter and cinnamon on low heat while cutting up biscuits into a non-stick Bundt pan. Pour mixture over the top and bake at 350 degrees for 30 minutes. Cover for first 10 minutes of baking with tin foil.

EGGNOG WAFFLES

2 cups biscuit mix (Bisquick)
¼ teaspoon nutmeg
1½ cups of eggnog
2 tablespoons salad oil
1 egg

Mix all ingredients thoroughly until smooth. A rotary mixer may be helpful. Pour into waffle maker or onto a griddle for a pancake-style.

FRENCH TOAST

2 cups milk
4 eggs
½ teaspoon salt
2 teaspoons cinnamon
Sliced bread

Beat four eggs thoroughly then mix all ingredients together. Dip bread into mixture until coated. Fry on an oiled griddle or skillet until golden brown.

FRESH SCRAMBLED EGGS FOR
THE ROOMMATES

12 eggs
2 tablespoons of butter
2 tablespoons of whipping cream
¼ teaspoon of salt
Pepper to taste

Combine eggs, salt and pepper and stir briskly. Use a fork or a whisk. Melt butter in a skillet, making sure it coats the bottom. Pour in the egg mixture and stir constantly while cooking over medium-low heat. The eggs should be firm yet moist. Remove from heat and stir in cream. Serves 5 roommates or 2 linemen from the football team.

HAM STEAK
(or Canadian Bacon)

1 pound ham steak or Canadian bacon
1 tablespoon of brown sugar
1 teaspoon of ground cloves
¼ cup of orange juice,
    fresh-squeezed if possible

Combine the juice, sugar and cloves into a sauce and pour into a baking dish. Lightly score the meat with a knife to allow sauce to seep in. Place meat in the dish and bake at 350 degrees for 40 to 45 minutes. Baste and turn occasionally. If you prefer the meat a little crisper, you can put it on a grill or in a fry pan.

HAM & EGG SCRAMBLE

1 package frozen fried potatoes
2 cups cubed ham
1 egg per person
1 small onion
Butter or margarine

Fry potatoes in butter and add diced or chopped onion. Beat eggs and pour over potato mixture. After eggs are pretty well cooked, add ham and cook on low for 15 minutes.

JUNGLE TOAST

2 slices of firm white bread
2 teaspoons of softened butter
1 large banana
½ teaspoon of sugar

Toast bread on one side using a broiler or toaster oven. Butter untoasted side. Coarsely mash banana with sugar and spread over butter. Run under broiler for 2 to 4 minutes to glaze. Carefully watch so corners don't burn.

LATE FOR CLASS BREAKFAST SHAKE

2 scoops of low fat yogurt
½ banana
½ cup fresh fruit of choice
1 cup of skim milk
2 ice cubes

Mix all ingredients in a blender. If you don't have a blender, put everything into a milk jug and shake.

OMELET IN A BAG

2 eggs
Onion, diced
Cheese, grated
Mushroom, sliced
¼ cup of ham, diced or 4 strips of bacon,
    cooked and crumbled

Boil water in a large pan. Crack 2 eggs into a quart-sized zip-lock bag. Add onion, cheese, mushroom, bacon or ham in desired amounts. Close the bag and remove excess air. Mix the ingredients by kneading the contents. Place the bag in boiling water for 15 to 18 minutes. Slide the omelet out of the bag and onto a plate.

OVEN OMELET

8 slices of bacon
8 eggs
1 cup of milk
½ teaspoon of salt
12 ounces of Monterey Jack cheese, shredded
4 green onions, chopped

Fry bacon and crumble. Beat eggs, milk, salt and 10 ounces of cheese together. Add in onions and bacon. Pour into a shallow baking dish Bake at 350 degrees for 30 to 40 minutes. Dish should be set and brown. Sprinkle remaining cheese and top and leave in oven until melted.

POP WAFFLES

2 cups biscuit mix
1 egg
3 tablespoons oil
1 1/3 cups of club soda or lemon-lime soda

Mix thoroughly. Pour into a pre-heated waffle iron or on griddle for pancake-style.

POTATO PANCAKES

4 cups mashed potatoes
1 tablespoon of flour

Mix potatoes and flour. Divide in half. On a floured surface, roll out each half to ¼-inch thickness. Cut mixture with round cookie cutter or a can with lid and bottom removed. Fry on un-greased pan until brown on both sides.

PUFFY FRENCH TOAST

1 cup of flour
1 cup of milk
2 eggs
1½ teaspoons of baking powder
½ teaspoon of salt
French bread

Mix the first five ingredients. Dip thick-sliced French bread into batter and fry until golden brown on both sides.

SPAM, EGGS & RICE

1 can of Spam
3 cups rice
8 eggs
Soy sauce

Cut Spam into ¼ inch slices. Brown both sides in skillet and set aside. Steam rice and set aside. Instant rice works best. Scramble 8 eggs in skillet. Put rice on plates, top with eggs and put Spam on the side. Sprinkle with soy sauce.

LUNCH

ALL-AMERICAN BURGER

2½ pounds of ground beef
  (the higher the grade the better)
2 tablespoons of olive oil or butter
Salt and freshly ground pepper to taste

Combine meat with salt and pepper and form into 6 patties. Melt butter or heat oil in a skillet or brush oil on the grill. Cook patties on medium-high heat for 4 to 6 minutes per side. Place on buns and pile on the toppings.

BACON BARBECUE BURGER

½ pound of ground beef
¼ cup of barbecue sauce
2 pineapple rings
4 strips of bacon
2 hamburger buns
Salt and pepper to taste

Combine ground beef with barbecue sauce and mix thoroughly. Season meat with salt and pepper. Form into 2 patties. Grill or broil for 4 to 6 minutes per side. Grill pineapple rings for 4 minutes. In a separate skillet, cook bacon until crispy. Top each meat patty with a pineapple ring and 2 pieces of bacon. Serve on toasted buns.

BACON CHEESE BBQ HOT DOGS

8 hot dogs
8 hot dog buns
8 slices of cheddar cheese
8 slices of bacon
½ cup of barbecue sauce
1 red onion, diced

Place bacon in a deep skillet. Cook over medium-high heat until browned and drain on paper towels.
In a separate pan or on a barbecue, grill hot dogs cook browned and fully cooked, or until done to your taste. Lightly toast or grill hot dog buns. Now place a slice of cheese and bacon on each roll. Add a hot dog and top each with 1 tablespoon of barbecue sauce and red onion.

BACON ROLL-UPS

½ cup of sour cream
½ teaspoon of onion salt
½ pound of bacon, cooked and crumbled
1 package of crescent rolls (8 ounce size)

Mix sour cream, onion salt and bacon then spread on the rolls and roll them up. Bake at 375 degrees for 12 to 15 minutes.

BARBECUE PORK BURGERS

2 pounds of ground pork
¼ cup fresh breadcrumbs
1 cup of barbecue sauce
6 burger buns
Salt and pepper (optional)

Mix ground pork with breadcrumbs and ½ cup of sauce to make six patties. Grill burgers on medium high heat, basting burgers often with remaining sauce. Takes about 10 minutes to cook, 5 minutes per side.

CASTLE OF WHITE MINI-BURGERS

1½ pounds of ground beef
1 egg
1 instant onion soup mix
½ cup diced onion
2 teaspoons water

Mix and press into a cookie sheet. Poke holes in meat placing diced onions in holes. Bake at 400 degrees for 10 minutes. Cut into squares use dinner rolls for buns.

BIG ISLAND BARBECUE BURGER

½ pound of ground beef
¼ cup of barbecue sauce
2 pineapple rings
4 strips of bacon
2 hamburger buns
Salt and pepper to taste

Combine ground beef with barbecue sauce and mix thoroughly. Season meat with salt and pepper. Form into 2 patties. Grill or broil for 4 to 6 minutes per side. Grill pineapple rings for 4 minutes. In a separate skillet, cook bacon until crispy. Top each meat patty with a pineapple ring and 2 pieces of bacon. Serve on toasted buns.

CRAB SANDWICH

8 ounces of canned or fresh crabmeat
8 ounces of Cheddar cheese, grated
1 cup of tomato soup
½ onion, grated
2 teaspoons of Miracle Whip or mayonnaise
Hamburger buns, bagels or English muffins

Mix all ingredients together and spread on bun, bagel or muffin halves. Bake at 350 degrees for 20 minutes. Recipe makes 10 to 12 sandwich halves.

DETROIT CONEY DOGS

4 natural casing hot dogs
4 hot dog buns, sliced
1 can of chili sauce without beans
1 onion, diced
4 tablespoons of mustard

Place hot dogs in a skillet or on a grill for 5 to 8 minutes. Lightly toast or grill the buns. Heat the chili sauce in a pan or microwave. Put the dogs in the buns and top with chili, onions and mustard.

DOGS WITH A KICK

1 package of hot dogs
1 can of jalapeno peppers
1 package of fresh carrots
1 onion, coarsely chopped
Corn chips

Cut hot dogs into bite-sized chunks. Cut carrots into ¼-inch thick slices. Put all ingredients in a slow cooker and heat until juice is reduced by half. Serve with corn chips.

FOILED HAMBURGER

1 pound of hamburger
1 onion
2 carrots
2 potatoes
Salt and pepper to taste

Make burger patties and place on aluminum foil. Thinly slice onions, carrots and potatoes and place on top of meat. Salt and pepper to taste. Fold foil into a pocket and fold edges over. Cook on grill or open fire.

GOLD MEDAL GRILLED CHEESE SANDWICH

3 ounces of softened cream cheese
¾ cup mayonnaise
1 cup shredded cheddar cheese
1 cup shredded mozzarella cheese
½ teaspoon garlic powder
1/8 teaspoon seasoning salt
10 slices of Italian bread (½ inch thick)
2 tablespoons butter

In a bowl, mix cream cheese and mayonnaise until smooth. Stir in cheese, garlic powder and seasoning salt. Spread 5 slices of bread with cheese mixture and top with remaining bread. Butter outside of sandwich and toast in a large pan or skillet for about 4 minutes a side or until golden brown.

GRILLED CHEESE AND PEAR SANDWICH

Sour Dough Bread (or your favorite)
Butter or Margarine
Sliced Sharp Cheddar
Sliced Havarti
Mayonnaise
Creamy Horse Radish Sauce
Bacon Bits
French's French Fried Onions
Pear Jam or Preserves
(peach or apricot work too)

For each sandwich butter one side of each slice of bread. On the other, spread one with a mixture of mayonnaise and horseradish sauce and one with the pear jam. Then between the 2 slices, add a slice of each cheese, bacon bits and French fried onions. Close and fry in pan until golden brown and cheese has melted.

GRILLED HAM AND CHEESE

2 slices of ham
1 slice of Swiss cheese
1 slice of salami
2 slices of whole wheat bread
1 tomato slices
1 teaspoon of Dijon mustard
Butter

Spread butter on one side of each bread slice. Spread mustard on the other side of each slice followed by salami, tomato, cheese and ham. Top with the second slice, butter-side up. Place sandwich in a large skillet on medium heat. Heat until cheese melts and bread is slightly toasted on one side. Flip sandwich and heat remaining side until toasted.

HUSKER HEAT BURGER

5 pounds of ground beef
3 tablespoons of mustard
4 ounces of ketchup
½ onion, chopped
1 teaspoon of salt
½ teaspoon of pepper
¼ teaspoon of red pepper flakes
4 tablespoons of horseradish
3 tablespoons of Worcestershire sauce
1 cup of water
Hamburger buns

Brown hamburger with chopped onion then drain the meat. Add horseradish, mustard, Worcestershire sauce, ketchup, salt, peppers and water. Simmer for 30 minutes. Scoop onto buns and serve.

PIZZA DOGS

4 hot dogs
4 hot dog buns, split
½ cup of marinara sauce
4 ounces of mozzarella, shredded
¼ cup of diced pepperoni

Cook the hot dogs on grill or in a skillet for 5 to 8 minutes, according to the package directions. Place a hot dog in each bun and, dividing evenly, top with the warmed marinara, pepperoni and mozzarella. Grill, bake or broil until the mozzarella has melted and browned, about 2 minutes.

QUESADILLA BURGER

6 ounces of ground beef
2 ounces of salsa
1 ounce shredded cheddar cheese
1 burger bun
Hot sauce (optional)

Grill the burger and place on the bun. Top with a few drops of hot sauce, salsa and cheese.

QUICK PIZZA

1 jar of tomato sauce
1 Package of shredded mozzarella cheese
1 Package of pepperoni
Bagels, bread or hamburger buns

Spread sauce on your bread of choice. Top with cheese and pepperoni. Bake at 375 degrees in an oven or toaster oven for 2 to 5 minutes. Keep an eye on it or you'll need the fire extinguisher.

ROAST BEEF SANDWICHES

2 cups of roast beef, cooked and thinly sliced
½ cup of honey
¼ cup of ketchup
¼ cup of apple cider vinegar
2 tablespoons of Worcestershire sauce
¼ teaspoon of maple extract

In a large skillet, mix ketchup, vinegar, honey, maple extract and Worcestershire sauce. Add sliced roast beef and simmer until steaming hot. Serve on French bread or hoagie rolls.

TURKEY HOAGIES

4 turkey breast fillets
4 hoagie buns
1 cup of soy sauce
1 cup of Sprite
1 cup of cooking oil

Combine soy sauce, Sprite and oil. Marinate fillets overnight. Grill the meat 6 to 8 minutes per side until browned. Baste with the marinade while cooking.

TURKEY BURGERS

1 pound of fresh ground turkey
¼ cup of chili sauce
1 teaspoon of chicken flavor bouillon powder

Combine ingredients, shape into patties and grill.

WALKING TACOS

1 small bag of corn chips (Fritos work best)
½ pound of ground beef, cooked
1 onion chopped
2 tomatoes, chopped
1 cup of salsa
1½ cups of shredded cheese, taco blend

Open bag of chips slightly and crush chips in bag. Now open bag completely and mix in the ingredients as you like. Sprinkle in hot sauce for the extra kick.

DINNER

ANGEL HAIR PASTA WITH SHRIMP

2 cans of chicken broth
¼ pound of fresh, cleaned shrimp
12 mushrooms chopped into quarters
1 sliced green onion
Angel hair pasta

Bring chicken broth to a boil the drop mushrooms in. Gently boil for 5 minutes. Add in the cleaned shrimp and boil for 3 minutes. Add in green onion and boil for another minute. Strain ingredients and add them into the pasta and toss. Pour broth over everything for desired flavor.

BAKED BEEF STEW

3 pound of beef cut into 1½-inch chunks
2 cans of cream of mushroom soup
¾ cup of wine or cooking sherry
½ envelope of dry onion soup mix

Mix all ingredients together in a baking dish and cover. Bake at 325 degrees for 3 hours or put in crock-pot and cook on "stew" setting.

BAKED CHICKEN BREASTS

4 chicken breasts
½ cup of Russian dressing
2 tablespoons of brown sugar
1 package of dried onion soup mix

Place chicken in a greased baking dish. Combine remaining ingredients and spread over chicken. Bake at 325 degrees for 45 minutes.

BARBECUED FISH

4 fish fillets
1 tablespoon cooking oil
Barbecue sauce
½ onion, diced
Bacon bits or 4 strips cooked & crumbled
Lemon pepper seasoning

Spread cooking oil in aluminum foil. Place fish fillets in foil and sprinkle with lemon pepper seasoning. Cover fillets with onion and bacon bits then cover with sauce. Place on grill or in oven at 350 degrees. Cook until fish is white and flaky. Dense fish like salmon may require higher heat and longer cooking time.

BEEF STEW & DUMPLINGS

24 ounce can of beef stew
1 10 to 12 ounce can of tomato soup
1 soup can water
1 cup Bisquick
1/3 cup of water

In a saucepan combine stew, soup and water. Bring to a boil. Mix Bisquick and 1/3 cup water and drop spoonfuls into boiling stew. Cook uncovered on low heat for 10 minutes. Cover and cook for 10 more minutes.

BEER CAN CHICKEN

4 to 5 pound chicken
3 tablespoons of oil (preferably olive oil)
1 half can of beer, room temperature
1 tablespoon of kosher salt or sea salt
1 tablespoon of dried thyme
1 tablespoon of black pepper

Rub the chicken with oil. Mix salt, pepper, thyme and sprinkle over chicken. Fire up the grill. When it reaches temperature, put the half empty can of beer on the grill, set up for indirect heat. Put chicken over the can so it is sitting upright, with the can in the cavity. Cover the grill. After one hour, check the chicken and refresh coals if needed. Using a meat thermometer, check every 15 minutes until the thickest part of the thigh reaches 160 to 165 degrees.

CHEDDAR BURGERS

1 egg
1 pound of ground beef
4 to 6 ounces of cheddar cheese, grated
1 teaspoon of salt
½ teaspoon
4 hamburger buns

Combine ingredients and form into four patties. Meat can be grilled, baked or fried in a pan with a tablespoon of oil. Never squeeze or push the meat with a spatula. It pushes out the juices and dries out the meat. Cook to desired doneness and serve on buns.

CHICKEN MAZATLAN

5 ounces of chicken breast
1 corn tortilla
2 tablespoons of salsa
2 tablespoons of green chilies
½ cup of Monterey Jack cheese
¼ cup of cheddar cheese

Cook the corn tortilla and put on the bottom of a plate. Add layers of green chilies, chicken, salsa, Monterey Jack and cheddar. Bake in oven or microwave until cheese is melted.

CHICKEN & MUSHROOM SOUP

2½ pounds of chicken pieces
2 cans of chicken mushroom soup
½ cup of milk
Parsley

Place chicken in a casserole or baking dish. Mix soup and milk and pour over chicken. Sprinkle with parsley and bake at 350 degrees for 90 minutes.

CHICKEN & RICE

1 small chicken
1 cup of raw rice
1 can of mushroom soup
1 can of celery soup
1 can of water

Put rice on the bottom of a baking dish then place chicken on the rice. Combine soups and a can of water and pour over chicken. Bake at 450 degrees for 20 minutes, and then reduce heat to 325 degrees for 1 hour and 20 minutes.

CHICKEN & RICE SOUP

6 cups of chicken broth
1 cup of rice
3 eggs, separated
1 lemon (juice)
Salt and pepper

Boil 6 cups of broth, add one cup of rice. Salt and pepper to taste. When rice is cooked, lower heat to a simmer. In a bowl, beat 3 egg whites until stiff. Slowly add yokes and juice from lemon. Beat well. Add broth a ladle at a time beating well into most of the broth is used. Pour mixture back into pot, stirring well. Chicken pieces may be added to soup.

CHICKEN PARMESAN

3 pounds of chicken pieces
1 cup of cornflakes, crushed
½ cup grated Parmesan cheese
¾ cup Miracle Whip

Combine corn flake crumbs and cheese. Coat chicken pieces with the Miracle Whip and then coat with crumb and cheese mixture. Put in dish and bake at 350 degrees for 60 minutes.

CHILI MEAT LOAF

2 pounds of ground beef
1 can of chili with beans
2 eggs, lightly beaten
1 medium onion, chopped

Mix ingredients and place into a greased shallow baking dish. Bake at 350 degrees for 90 minutes.

CORN FLAKE CHICKEN

1 chicken in parts
4 cups corn flakes
½ cup evaporated milk
½ cup butter
1 teaspoon of salt
1/8 teaspoon of pepper

Crush corn flakes into crumbs and mix with salt and pepper. Dip chicken pieces in milk and roll in seasoned crumbs. Place chicken pieces skin side up in a single layer in pan. Drizzle with melted butter. Bake at 350 degrees for 60 minutes.

CREAM OF BROCCOLI SOUP

1 package of chopped broccoli
½ cup of grated cheddar cheese
1 can of cream of mushroom soup
1 can of water
¼ teaspoon of thyme
Red pepper

Mix ingredients except cheese in a pot. Cover and simmer for 10 minutes. Add cheese and stir.

DIXIE CHICKEN

1 can of condensed tomato soup
2 tablespoons of honey
1 teaspoon of dry mustard
½ teaspoon of onion powder
4 chicken breast halves, skinned

Mix soup, honey, dry mustard and onion powder. Place chicken on a rack in a broiler pan. Broil 6 inches from heat for 30 minutes or until no longer pink. Brush with soup mixture, turning often.

EMPTY THE PANTRY STEAK

3 pounds of meat (ground beef, pork, etc.)
1 cup of cracker crumbs
1 cup of water
1 can of cream of mushroom soup
Salt and pepper

Combine meat, cracker crumbs and water. Season to taste. Form into patties and brown in skillet. Remove from pan and put in an oven roaster. Spread soup over the meat and bake covered.

FAST CHICKEN SOUP

3 cups of water
3 chicken bouillon cubes
2 carrots, chopped
2 celery stalks, chopped
1 cup of chicken, chopped and cooked
    (leftover works great)

In a pan, bring water to a boil and add carrots, celery and bouillon. Reduce heat and let simmer for 10 minutes. Add chopped chicken and simmer for 3 more minutes.

FIVE CAN HOT DISH

1 can of mushroom soup
1 can of chicken soup
1 large can of tuna
1 small can of evaporated milk
1 can of chow mien noodles
1 cup of finely chopped celery

Combine all ingredients and bake at 350 degrees for 1 hour.

FIVE FINGER CASSEROLE

1 pound of hamburger
¼ cup of diced onion
4 medium sliced potatoes
¾ cup of shredded cheese
½ cup of flour

Brown hamburger and onion in a pan. Sprinkle ½ cup of flour on the mixture and make a thick gravy. Add cheese and pour over sliced potatoes in a casserole dish and bake at 325 degrees for 90 minutes.

FOILED FISH

4 fish fillets, ¼ pound to ½ pound each,
    cleaned and de-boned
1 onion, diced
1 stalk of celery (celery salt can be used)
1 green pepper, diced
4 pats of butter
Salt and pepper

Place each fillet on a piece of aluminum foil big enough to fully wrap each fish. Add in onion, green pepper and celery (or celery salt). Salt and pepper to taste. Top with a pat of butter. Wrap tightly and bake directly on hot coals or grill for 15 to 20 minutes. This makes for a great campfire dinner.

FRATERNITY CHOWDER

3 pounds of potatoes, peeled and cubed
32 ounces of canned corn, whole kernel
32 ounces of creamed corn
4 bunches of green onions, chopped
5 cups of chicken broth or bullion
5 cups of water
4 cups of milk, 2% or skim
2 tablespoons of oil

In a large skillet, brown onions in oil. Add a little bit of the broth and simmer for 2 minutes. Add remaining chicken broth, water, milk and potatoes. Simmer until potatoes are tender. Add corn and cook for an additional 2 minutes. Blend until smooth and creamy.

FRENCH ONION SOUP

4 cups of chicken broth
1 large Bermuda onion
½ stick of butter
¼ cup of Sauterne wine

Slice onion thinly and sauté in butter until lightly browned. Add chicken broth, simmer and season to taste. When ready to serve add in wine.

GRILLED PORK CHOPS

4 1-inch thick pork chops
¼ teaspoon of salt
¾ teaspoon of lemon pepper
½ teaspoon of whole, dried oregano leaves

Mix salt, lemon pepper and oregano and coat the pork chops. Grill over low to medium heat for 25 minutes or until chops are no longer pink. Turn them once.

HAWAIIAN CHICKEN

1 small bottle of Italian dressing
1 small jar of apricot preserves
1 package of Lipton onion soup mix
5 boneless chicken breasts

Mix all ingredients together and pour over chicken. Bake at 350 degrees for 20 to 30 minutes.

HONEY BARBECUE CHICKEN

3 pounds of chicken
3 tablespoons of honey
3 tablespoons of mustard
1 tablespoon of sesame seeds

Barbecue chicken on the grill or bake in the oven. Mix honey, mustard and sesame seeds. Ten minutes before taking off the heat, brush the chicken with the mixture.

ITALIAN FISH FILLETS

2 pounds of fish fillets, fresh or thawed
8 ounces of spaghetti sauce with mushrooms
2 tablespoons of chopped onion
1 cup of shredded mozzarella cheese
Salt

Place fillets on a greased baking sheet. Salt to taste. Mix spaghetti sauce with onion and pour over fish. Bake uncovered at 350 degrees for 25 to 30 minutes, or until fish flakes easily. Sprinkle with cheese and bake for another 3 minutes or until cheese is melted.

KRAUT DOGS

8 quarter-pound hot dogs
2 cups of sauerkraut
2 tablespoons of brown sugar
8 tablespoons of brown mustard
8 hot dog buns, toasted

Cut the dogs almost in half and grill on a barbecue or in a pan. While dogs are being cooked, mix sauerkraut and brown sugar and heat in a small pan. Keep stirring the mixture. When cooked, place dogs on the buns and drizzle a tablespoon of mustard on each. Top with sauerkraut and dig in!

LASAGNA

1 pound of hamburger, browned
1 quart of spaghetti sauce
1 box of lasagna noodles
1 pint of cottage cheese
1 pound of grated Swiss cheese
1 pound of grated Mozzarella
¾ cup of water
Parmesan cheese

In an 8-inch by 14-inch pan layer sauce, hamburger, uncooked noodles, cottage cheese and Swiss cheese. Repeat layers and finish with Mozzarella cheese. Add the water and sprinkle with Parmesan cheese. Bake at 350 degrees for one hour or until noodles are cooked.

LAZY MEATLOAF

1 pound of meat (your choice on this one)
1 egg
1 box of stuffing
1 cup of water

Mix all ingredients together and put into loaf pan. Cook at 350 degrees for 45 minutes.

LEAVE IT ALONE STEW

1½ pounds of meat (beef, chicken or pork)
1 cup of ginger ale
1 can of cream of mushroom soup
1 small can of mushrooms, chopped
1 package of dry onion soup mix

Mix all ingredients and pour into a tightly covered 9-inch by 12-inch baking dish. Bake at 350 degrees for 2¾ to 3 hours. Resist peeking.

MAC & CHEESE

1½ cups of uncooked macaroni
3 cups of milk
2 cups of sharp cheddar cheese

Spray a casserole dish with non-stick spray. Mix macaroni, milk and cheese and pour into dish. Bake at 325 degrees for 75 minutes.

MAC & CHEESE DELUXE

8 ounces of macaroni shells
8 ounces of sour cream
1 egg, lightly beaten
2 cups of cottage cheese, small curd
2 cups of shredded American cheese
2 teaspoons of butter
¼ cup of soft breadcrumbs
¼ teaspoon of salt
¼ teaspoon of pepper

Cook macaroni according to the package directions and drain. Combine macaroni, egg, cottage cheese, sour cream, salt, pepper and cheeses and stir well. Pour mixture into a greased baking dish. Combine breadcrumbs and butter, stir well, and sprinkle over macaroni. Bake at 300 degrees for 30 minutes.

MEATLOAF

1½ pounds of ground beef
1¾ teaspoons of salt
1 egg, beaten
1 cup of ketchup
¾ cup of uncooked oats
¼ cup of diced onion

Combine all ingredients thoroughly and press into an ungreased loaf pan. Bake at 350 degrees for 1 hour. Let stand for 5 to 10 minutes before cutting.

MUSHROOM AND SHRIMP KABOBS

1 pound of fresh shrimp, cleaned
½ pound of fresh mushrooms
¼ pound of butter
4 tablespoons of butter

In a small pan, slowly melt butter and stir in lemon juice.   Let liquid cool. Marinate shrimp and mushroom caps in the mixture for 20 minutes. Alternate shrimp and mushrooms onto wooden skewers. Place on a medium-hot grill or in an oven at 375 degrees. For oven cooking, place on rack with a cookie sheet underneath to catch drippings. Cook for 10 minutes.

NUTS & RICE BURGER

½ cup of walnuts
¾ cup of cooked rice
½ onion, diced
1 tablespoon of vegan bacon bits
  (Bac'Uns and McCormick's work well)
¼ teaspoon of garlic powder
4 teaspoons of oil
Salt and pepper to taste
Flour
4 hamburger buns

Grind walnuts and cooked rice in a blender or food processor. Sauté diced onion in 2 tablespoons of oil until it is tender and combine with walnuts, rice, garlic powder and vegan bacon bits in a bowl. Salt and pepper to taste. Shape into 4 patties and chill for 2 hours in the refrigerator. Add 2 tablespoons of oil to a skillet. Grill on medium high heat for 4 to 5 minutes per side or cook on a barbecue. Tastes great on gluten-free buns.

OLD COLLEGE TRY CHILI

2½ pounds of ground beef
1 cup of onion, diced
2 teaspoons of chili powder
1 teaspoon of mustard
½ cup of ketchup
1 teaspoon of salt
½ teaspoon of oregano
1 cup of water
1 can of pinto beans
1 can of red kidney beans
½ teaspoon of pepper
Hot sauce to taste

Brown meat in a skillet. Place meat and remaining ingredients in a pot and stir thoroughly. Cover pot and simmer for 2 hours.

ONION SOUP

3 onions, sliced thin
2 tablespoons of butter
6 cups of chicken broth
¼ teaspoon of pepper

Warm butter in a large pan. Be careful not to scorch. Add in onions and sauté until browned. Add broth and pepper. Bring to a boil. Reduce heat and simmer for 20 minutes.

ONION PORK CHOPS

8 pork chops
4 potatoes, peeled
1½ envelopes of dry onion soup mix
2 cups of water

Brown pork chops in a skillet and blot with paper towels to remove grease. Splice potatoes thin and layer in a baking dish. Place pork chops on potatoes. Combine soup mix and water and pour over chops and potatoes. Cover with foil and bake at 350 degrees for 75 minutes.

ORANGE CHICKEN

3 pounds of chicken parts
4 tablespoon of orange juice concentrate
4 tablespoons of butter
Salt and pepper

Divide chicken parts up into four servings. Put each serving on a piece of heavy-duty aluminum foil and form into a pouch. Season with salt and pepper to taste. Pour a tablespoon of juice and a pat of butter in each foil pouch. Wrap up tightly. Bake on a grill over hot coals for about an hour or place pouches on a baking sheet in an oven at 350 degrees for one hour.

PORK CHOP CASSEROLE

6 pork chops
4 potatoes
2 cans of green beans
2 cans of cream of mushroom soup

Brown pork chops in a skillet then place them in the bottom of a baking dish. Slice potatoes thick and place on top of the pork chops. Now layer green beans and top with soup. Bake at 375 degrees for 1 hour.

QUICK BARBECUED FISH

8 fish fillets, cleaned and de-boned
2 cups of French dressing
3 cups of cracker crumbs

Dip fillets in dressing and coat with cracker crumbs. Put fillets on a grill about 5 inches from the coals. Brush with more dressing. Cook 3 to 4 minutes per side but be careful not to over cook. You can also bake in the oven at 350 degrees for 12 to 20 minutes.

ROUND STEAK & GRAVY

2 to 2 ½ pounds of round steak
1 package of onion soup mix
¼ cup water
1 can of condensed cream of mushroom soup

Cut steak into 5 to 6 pieces. Place in slow cooking pot or slow cooker. Add dry on onion soup mix, water and condensed mushroom soup. Cover and cook on low 6 to 8 hours.

SAUSAGE STEW

½ pound of sausage
1 chopped onion
1 can of black-eyed peas
1 can of hominy
1 can of pinto beans (optional)
1 can of whole corn

Brown sausage and onion. Add in remaining ingredients but do not drain vegetables. Simmer over low heat for 30 minutes. Salt and pepper to taste. You can also use Spam or hamburger in place of sausage.

SLOPPY JOE'S

½ pound of hamburger
1-pound can of beans
¼ cup of ketchup
Oil
Butter
Barbecue sauce to taste

In a skillet, sauté hamburger in a little butter and oil with medium heat until it loses color. Mix beans and burger in ketchup and barbecue sauce. Simmer uncovered for 5 minutes. Spoon mixture onto split, buttered and toasted hamburger buns.

SOUPED UP FISH

1 pound of fresh fish
1 can of cream of mushroom soup
¼ cup of apple juice
¼ teaspoon of curry powder

Place fish in a baking dish. Combine soup, apple juice and curry powder and pour over fish. Bake at 350 degrees for 15 to 20 minutes.

SPLIT PEA SOUP

½ pound of bacon
5 cups of water
1 cup of milk
10 ounces of split peas (dry)
1 carrot, chopped
1 teaspoon of salt

In a large pan, cook bacon on medium heat. Remove bacon when done and drain the grease. Combine water and split peas in the pan. Simmer on medium uncovered for 45 minutes. If mixture gets too thick, add a little more water. Stir in carrots and bacon and simmer for 20 more minutes. Stir in milk and salt and heat until piping hot.

STEAK STIR FRY

3 small steaks, cut into strips
¼ cup of carrots, sliced
¼ cup of onion, sliced
¼ cup of celery, diced
¼ cup of peas
¼ cup of bell pepper, diced
1 small can of water chestnuts
Stir-fry sauce

Fry steak strips in a pan until almost done. Add vegetables and let simmer for 1 to 2 minutes. Add stir-fry sauce to taste. Cook until vegetables are done but crispy. Serve on white rice.

STRAIGHT "A" ROAST

3 pound roast (beef, pork or deer)
2 cups of fresh brewed coffee
2 cans of cream of mushroom soup
1 package of dry onion soup mix
Salt and pepper

Flour and brown meat in a skillet. Put roast in a crock-pot with remaining ingredients. Cook for 8 hours. This recipe is very effective for tough meat.

SWEET AND SOUR RIBS

2 pounds of ribs, country-style or baby back
1 large onion, sliced
2 green peppers, sliced
½ cup of brown sugar
½ cup of vinegar
2 tablespoons of soy sauce
2 tablespoons of cornstarch
½ cup of water
½ teaspoon of salt
1 chicken bouillon cube

Put ribs in a baking dish or small roasting pan. Put onion and green peppers on the meat. Put the remaining ingredients in a pan, mix thoroughly, and bring to a boil. Pour this sauce over the meat and bake at 350 degrees for 1 hour. For a shortcut, boil the meat in water for 5 minutes. Then cover meat with two cups of your favorite barbecue sauce and bake at 350 degrees for 1 hour.

TACO HOT DISH

1½ pounds of hamburger
½ large onion, diced
10 ounces of tomato juice
4 ounces of canned chilies
1 large bag of tortilla chips
Grated cheese
Salt and pepper

Brown meat and onion in a pan. Add the chilies and tomato juice and heat until hot. In a baking dish or pan, crush ¾ of the chips and layer them on the bottom. Pour the meat mixture on top. Add as much grated cheese as you like and top with the remaining crushed chips. Bake at 350 degrees for 30 minutes. Serve with hot sauce or taco sauce.

TACO SOUP

1 pound of hamburger, browned
30 ounces of canned or fresh tomatoes
1 can of kidney beans
1 can of tomato soup
2 cups of water
1 package of taco seasoning

Combine all ingredients. Bring to a boil and then simmer for 30 minutes.

TATER TOT CASSEROLE

1 pound of lean ground beef
3 tablespoons of Worcestershire Sauce
16 ounces of cheddar cheese
1 can of mushroom soup
1 package of mixed vegetables
1 package of tater tots

Mix beef, soup and Worcestershire sauce in a baking dish. Cover with vegetables and layer with cheddar cheese. Top with tater tots. Bake at 350 degrees for 45 minutes.

TUNA BURGER

1 can of tuna fish
1 egg
½ cup of cracker crumbs
¼ cup of milk
¼ teaspoon of onion flakes
¼ teaspoon of oregano
Salt and pepper to taste
Cheddar cheese
Tomato slices
Lettuce
Oil
Hamburger buns

Mix fish, egg, cracker crumbs, milk, onion, oregano, salt and pepper then form into patties. Fry in skillet. Top with cheese, tomato and lettuce and serve on buttered, toasted hamburger buns.

SNACKS &
SIDES

ALL-NIGHTER NACHOS

2 green onions, diced
½ bag of tortilla chips
1 cup of cheese, shredded
2 ounces of olives, sliced
2 tablespoons of sour cream
1 can of refried beans
Salsa

Pour chips in a baking dish. Spread refried beans evenly over the chips and sprinkle with grated cheese. Bake mixture at 350 degrees for 10 to 15 minutes or until cheese is melted. When it's time to serve top with salsa, olives green onions and sour cream.

BACON ROLL-UPS

½ cup of sour cream
½ teaspoon of onion salt
½ pound of bacon, cooked and crumbled
1 package of crescent rolls (8 ounce size)

Mix sour cream, onion salt and bacon then spread on the rolls and roll them up. Bake at 375 degrees for 12 to 15 minutes.

BAKED BEANS

5 slices of bacon, shredded into small pieces
1 large onion, diced
1 large can baked beans
1/3 cup of brown sugar
½ cup ketchup

Cook bacon and onion until onion is soft and meat is mostly cooked without being crisp. Drain grease. Mix in remaining ingredients thoroughly. Bake mixture at 350 degrees for 60 minutes.

BAKED CORN

2 cans of cream style corn
3 eggs
½ cup of sugar
3 tablespoons of melted butter
2½ tablespoons of flour
¾ cup of milk

Mix together all ingredients except milk and flour. Mix flour and milk together until the lumps disappear. Combine all ingredients and pour into a greased baking dish. Bake at 375 degrees for 90 minutes. Do not put a lid on the dish.

BAR CHEESE

2 pounds of Velveeta cheese
6 ounces of horseradish
8 drops of Tabasco sauce
1 cup of mayonnaise

Combine cheese, Tabasco sauce and horseradish in a double boiler. If you don't have a double boiler, put ingredients in a small pot and place in a larger pot half-filled with water. Once melted, remove from heat and add mayonnaise. Mix thoroughly. Pour into a container and let cool.

BARBECUE PARTY SAUSAGE

1 pound of smoked Polish sausage
1 can of whole mushrooms
½ bottle of KC Masterpiece Barbecue Sauce
    (or the sauce brand of your choice)

Bake and drain sausage and cut into bite-size chunks. Combine all ingredients, warm and serve.

BEER BREAD

3 cups self-rising flour
3 tablespoons sugar
1 can of beer
3 tablespoons melted butter

Combine ingredients thoroughly and pour into a greased loaf pan. Bake at 350 degrees for 45 minutes or until golden brown. Brush/drizzle melted butter on top.

CHEESE SAUCE

3 tablespoons of butter
3 tablespoons of flour
½ cup of grated cheese of choice
1 cup of milk, whole or 2%
Salt and pepper

Melt butter in a small pan. Add flour gradually and stir until smooth. Slowly add milk and continue to stir. Once the mixture is smooth, add cheese and continue to stir until the cheese is completely melted. Salt and pepper to taste.

CHEESY RICE

3 cups of cooked rice
½ cup of sour cream
1 teaspoon of salt
2 dashes of ground red pepper
1 cup of grated cheddar cheese
Butter

Combine cooked rice, sour cream, salt, ½ cup of cheese and red pepper to taste. Spoon into a buttered baking dish. Top with remaining ½ cup of cheese. Bake at 350 degrees for 20 minutes.

CHICKEN CHUNKS

4 chicken breasts, boneless & skinless
1 bottle of ranch dressing
Crushed cornflakes
Red pepper flakes (optional)

Crush corn flakes in a bowl. Pour dressing in a second bowl. Cut chicken breasts into chunks. Dip chicken into dressing and then roll in cornflakes. For an extra kick, combine pepper flakes with corn flakes. Put the chicken chunks on a cookie sheet. Bake at 375 degrees for 7 to 9 minutes.

CHILI DIP

8 ounces of cream cheese
1 can of chili (no beans)
½ cup of grated cheddar cheese

Place cream cheese in the bottom of a microwaveable baking dish. Cover with chili and top with grated cheese. Heat in the microwave on high for 3 minutes or until cheese melts.

CHINESE MEATBALLS

1½ pounds ground beef
½ cup rice, washed
1 teaspoon of salt
½ teaspoon pepper
1 tablespoon of onion, minced
1 small can tomato soup

Combine beef, rice, salt, pepper and onion, shape into small balls. Heat tomato soup with ½ cup of water in a pan. Drop meatballs into soup mixture and cover. Simmer for one hour.

COLA CHICKEN WINGS

2 pounds of chicken wings
1 12-ounce can of cola (or cherry cola)
1 cup of ketchup
1 tablespoon Worcestershire (optional)

Place wings in a pan. Mix the ingredients thoroughly and pour over wings. Cook at 375 degrees for about 60 minutes while occasionally stirring to keep wings glazed.

COLE SLAW

1 head of cabbage, shredded
3 carrots, shredded
2 cups of Mayonnaise
  (Hellman's or Best Foods brand)
1 teaspoon of celery seed
1/3 cup of sugar
¼ cup of white vinegar

Mix mayonnaise, celery seed, sugar and vinegar. Make sure sugar dissolves. Toss mixture with cabbage and carrots. Refrigerate overnight.

CORNBREAD DELUXE

2 packages of Jiffy Corn Muffin mix
4 eggs
1 cup of oil
1 cup of sour cream
2 tablespoons of minced onion
1 can of cream style corn

Beat eggs, oil and sour cream together. Add in corn and onion. Stir muffin mix in quickly. Bake in a greased 9-inch by 13-inch pan at 350 degrees for 40 minutes.

DIRTY RICE

1 cup of uncooked white rice
1 stick of butter or margarine
1 can of onion soup
1 can of beef or chicken bouillon

Mix ingredients in a baking dish. Cover and bake at 350 degrees for 1 hour.

EGG SALAD

6 hard-boiled eggs, chopped
½ cup of celery, chopped
¼ cup of green pepper, diced
1 tablespoon of pimento, chopped (optional)
½ cup of mayonnaise or Miracle Whip
½ teaspoon of salt
¼ teaspoon of pepper

Combine all ingredients and mix thoroughly. Serve on its own or as a sandwich spread.

FIVE-CUP SALAD

1 cup of pineapple bits, drained
1 cup of mandarin oranges, drained
1 cup of miniature marshmallows
1 cup of shredded coconut
1 cup of sour cream

Combine all ingredients and refrigerate overnight.

FRIED GREEN TOMATOES

½ cup of flour
4 medium tomatoes cut into thick slices
4 tablespoons of oil or bacon grease
Salt and pepper

Cover tomato slices in flour and fry in hot grease. Turn slices to brown both sides. Add salt and pepper to taste.

FRUIT DIP

8 ounces of softened cream cheese
¼ cup of butterscotch ice cream topping
1 tablespoon of brown sugar
1 teaspoon of vanilla

Combine all ingredients in a bowl. Serve with your favorite fruit.

GARLIC CHEESES BREAD

½ pound of softened butter or margarine
½ pound of cheddar cheese, grated
¼ cup of Romano cheese, grated
¼ teaspoon of garlic powder
1 loaf of sliced French bread

Mix first 4 ingredients together and spread thickly on French bread slices. Place under a broiler, or in an oven on broil, until cheese is melted.

GREEN BEAN CASSEROLE

1 can of green beans
1 can of cream of mushroom soup
1 cup of grated cheese
16 Ritz crackers, crushed

Drain green beans and spread in a casserole dish. Now pour on the soup, sprinkle the cheese and top with cracker crumbs. Bake at 350 degrees for 30 minutes.

HANGOVER BARS

1 cup of Karo syrup
1 cup of sugar
1 cup of peanut butter
6 cups of Special K cereal
1 cup of chocolate, vanilla or
    butterscotch chips

Mix syrup and sugar in a pan and bring to a boil. Remove from heat and add peanut butter and Special K. Press the mixture into a greased 9-inch by 9-inch pan. Melt chips of choice and pour over cereal mix. Consume after a night of over-indulging in strong drink.

HAWAIIAN WINGS

3 pounds of chicken wings
½ cup of soy sauce
½ cup of coconut syrup
½ of thawed frozen orange juice concentrate

Cut through each full wing to make two pieces, Line a baking sheet with foil. Combine ingredients and pour half over chicken. Bake at 400 degrees for 15 to 20 minutes. Turn chicken and pour remaining sauce over chicken. Bake for another 15 to minutes.

HEART STOPPING WEENIES

1 package of Hillshire Farms Lil Smokies
1 package of bacon
½ cup of brown sugar
Toothpicks

Cut bacon into pieces big enough to wrap around weenies and sugar with a toothpick. Top each one with ½ teaspoon of brown sugar. Put them on a cookies sheet and bake for 20 minutes at 400 degrees. When serving, keep a cardiologist's phone number handy just in case.

HOMEMADE POTATO CHIPS

3 large potatoes
Vegetable oil
Salt

Slice potatoes paper thin to about one-sixteenth of an inch. Place slices in ice water until you are ready to fry. In a deep fryer or pan, heat oil to 375 degrees. Place 6 to 8 slices on paper towels to dry then slide slices one at a time into the oil. Fry 8 slices at a time until golden brown. Drain on paper towel and salt. You can also try celery or garlic salt.

KITCHEN SINK TRAIL MIX

½ cup of banana chips
1 cup of Rice Chex
¼ cup of chocolate or vanilla chips
½ cup of raisins or craisins
1 cup of mini pretzels
1 cup of Cheerios
¼ cup of cashews
¼ cup of almond slivers
½ cup of dried apple
¼ cup of dried apricot

Put all ingredients in a paper bag and shake thoroughly. Pour into a bowl and serve. Measurements are just an example, adjust to taste.

MEATBALLS

2 pounds of hamburger
1 cup of milk
1 egg, beaten
1 package of dry onion soup mix
2 slices of fresh bread, cut into small pieces

Mix all ingredients together and form into balls. Arrange on a cookie sheet or roasting pan and broil for 10 to 15 minutes.

MUSHROOM & ONION RICE

½ cup of butter
1 box of minute rice
2 cans of French onion soup
8 ounces of mushrooms, canned or fresh

Melt butter in a pan. Add minute rice and mix. Stir in soup and mushrooms. Put everything in a casserole dish and bake at 350 degrees for 30 minutes.

NACHO CHEESE DIP

1 pound of Velveeta cheese
1 can of chili without beans

Heat in a pan, crock-pot or fondue pot, stirring occasionally.

NO BAKE GRANOLA BARS

½ cup corn syrup
½ cup peanut butter
2 cups granola cereal
¼ cup raisins
¼ cup peanuts (or nut of choice)

Combine granola, raisins and nuts and mix well. Heat corn syrup to a boil and blend in peanut butter. Immediately pour over granola mixture and mix quickly to coat. Press firmly into an 8-inch square pan. Cool before cutting into bars. Makes a dozen hefty bars.

OATMEAL HEALTH BARS

1 cup of butter
1 cup of brown sugar, packed
¼ teaspoon of baking soda
½ cup of wheat germ
4 cups of oats, quick or standard

Boil sugar, soda, butter and wheat germ together. Remove from heat and stir in oats. Spread in a baking pan. Bake at 375 degrees for 10 minutes. After it cools cut into squares.

ONION ROASTED POTATOES

2 pounds of potatoes cut into chunks
1 envelope of dried onion soup mix
1/3 cup of oil (I prefer olive oil)

Mix oil and soup together in a Ziploc bag. Add in potatoes and shake to coat. Place potatoes on a cookie sheet and bake at 450 degrees for 40 minutes. Stir occasionally.

OVEN JERKY

4 pounds of beef
1¾ cups brown sugar
4 ounces of meat cure
3½ ounces soy sauce
3 tablespoons liquid smoke
4 cloves minced garlic

Cut meat into ¼ inch strips, removing fat. Combine ingredients in a Ziploc bag. Once mixed, put meat in bag and seal it. Place in fridge for 12 hours; knead every 2 to 3 hours. Remove meat from bag, wash and towel dry. Put on oven rack at low heat for 11 to 12 hours.

PASTA SALAD

7 ounces of pasta, cooked and drained
1 cup of chopped potatoes
1 cup of diced ham
1 green onion, cut into strips
1 small onion, cut into strips
2 cups of Italian dressing

Combine all ingredients. Cover and chill for at least 3 hours then serve.

PIZZA CRACKERS

4 dozen crackers
1 cup of pizza or spaghetti sauce
2 ounces of pepperoni
1 cup of finely shredded mozzarella

Spread sauce on crackers and top with pepperoni. Sprinkle with cheese and bake on a cookie sheet at 400 degrees for 3 to 5 minutes.

POTATO CAKES

6 potatoes
½ cup of milk
1 cup of flour
2 teaspoons of salt
2 eggs
Shortening

Grate potatoes medium fine. Combine with milk, eggs, flour and salt. Drop spoonfuls into hot lard and flatten. Cook until brown of both sides.

PRETZEL PARTY MIX

8 ounces of mini-pretzels (sticks or pieces)
1 cup of butter
1 cup of margarine
2 tablespoons of Worcestershire sauce
4 cups of Corn Chex
4 cups of Cheerios
4 cups of mini-Shredded wheat (or frosted)
4 cups of Life cereal
2 cups of Cheese-Its
1 cup of salted peanuts (optional)
Garlic powder, Cheddar powder to taste

Melt butter and margarine in a baking pan. Stir in Worcestershire sauce. Add in all other ingredients, except peanuts and powders. Toss to coat. Add in peanuts and mix. Sprinkle with garlic and cheese powder. Bake at 200 degrees for 2½ hours. Stir every 30 minutes. If needed, season with additional cheese powder.

RAMEN NOODLE SALAD

½ head of cabbage, shredded
4 chopped green onions
1 package of ramen noodles
2 tablespoons of sesame seeds, toasted
½ cup of slivered almonds, toasted
Dressing of choice

Toss cabbage, green onions and dressing together. Add remaining ingredients and serve.

REUBEN SLIDERS

1½ cups of corned beef, chopped
1 cup of sauerkraut
½ cup of shredded Swiss cheese
½ cup of Thousand Island dressing
1 loaf of thin-sliced cocktail rye

In a bowl combine corned beef, drained sauerkraut, shredded Swiss cheese and Thousand Island dressing. Mix well. Place mini-sandwiches on a baking sheet and bake at 375 degrees for 10 to 12 minutes or until cheese is melted.

ROASTED POTATOES

2½ pounds red potatoes
¼ cup olive oil
2 teaspoons salt
¼ teaspoon paprika
½ teaspoon pepper

Rinse, dry and chop potatoes into cubes. Combine oil, salt, paprika and pepper. Mix well. Add potatoes and toss. Place on an oiled tray. Bake at 425 degrees for 45 minutes until tender and well browned. Turn every 15 minutes.

SALAD DRESSING

¾ cup Miracle Whip or Mayonnaise
¼ cup ketchup

Whip together. For a richer flavor mix ingredients in a 1:1 ratio. Diced sweet pickle is optional.

SALAMI WRAPS

1 package of dry salami slices
1 can of chopped olives
1 carton of whipped cream cheese
Toothpicks

Mix cream cheese and chopped olives to your taste. Spread the mixture lightly in a salami piece. Roll up the salami and secure with a toothpick.

SAUSAGE BALLS

2 pounds of sausage (chopped or diced)
3 cups of Bisquick
1 large jar of Cheez Whiz

Mix all ingredients in a bowl. Form into 1-inch balls and bake at 350 degrees for 15 minutes.

STEAMED RICE

1 cup of long-grain rice (not instant)
2 ½ cups of water
1 teaspoon of salt
Butter

Pour water into a small pan, add salt and bring to a boil. Add rice and cover pan. Reduce the heat to medium. Cook 20 to 25 minutes or until all of the water is absorbed. Add butter to taste (optional).

SPICED WILD RICE

4 cups of cooked wild rice
1 cup of sour cream
½ teaspoon of nutmeg
¼ cup of water chestnuts, chopped

Prepare 1 cup of raw, uncooked wild rice according to directions on the package. This will fluff up to about 4 cups. Once cooked, add sour cream, nutmeg and water chestnuts. Serve hot.

STUFFED PEPPERS

1 can of chili (with no beans)
4 bell peppers
1 can of corn (drained)
Tortilla chips
Hot sauce (optional)

Cut the tops of the peppers and remove the insides. Boil in water for 12 to 15 minutes and drain. In a pan combine chili and corn and heat until cooked. Fill peppers with the mixture and hot sauce. Serve peppers with chips.

SUMMER SALAD

3 tomatoes
2 cucumbers
2 celery stalks
2 green onions
¼ cup of mayonnaise

Cut tomatoes into wedges. Slice cucumbers, celery and onions. Mix vegies together with mayonnaise. Salt and pepper to taste if you like.

TACO SNACK MIX

4 cups of Chex cereal
4 cups of pretzels (sticks or mini)
4 cups of tortilla chips
1 package of taco seasoning
¼ cup of margarine or butter

In a bowl mix Chex cereal, pretzels, tortilla chips and seasoning. Mix evenly then drizzle melted margarine or butter and toss until evenly coated.

THREE BEAN SALAD

1 can of kidney beans
1 can of garbanzo beans
1 can of green beans
1 small red onion, chopped
½ cup of Italian dressing

Mix ingredients and refrigerate for at least 2 hours.

WALDORF SALAD

4 cups of chopped apples
¾ cup of raisins
½ cup of pecan pieces
½ cup of mayonnaise

Combine all ingredients and refrigerate until you are
ready to serve.

DESSERTS

ANTS ON A LOG

Celery Stalks
Peanut Butter
Raisins

Wash celery and cut into halves. Spread peanut butter on the middle of each piece of celery. Place a few raisins on each half to look like "ants."

APPLE COBBLER

1 stick of margarine
1 cup of flour
2/3 cup of sugar
2 cans of apple pie filling

Take margarine, sugar and flour and mix well. Pour apple pie filling into a 9-inch by 13-inch pan. Crumble above mixture over the top and bake at 350 degrees for 1 hour or until golden brown. Recipe also works with cherry pie filling.

APPLE CRISP

5 cups of sliced apples
¾ cup of flour
1 teaspoon of cinnamon
1 cup of brown sugar
¾ cup of rolled oats
½ cup of butter

Arrange apples in a buttered pan. Combine sugar, flour, oats and cinnamon. Cut in butter until crumbly. Press over apples. Bake at 350 degrees for about 45 minutes.

BLACK & WHITE PEANUTS

1 large package of milk chocolate chips
1 large package of vanilla chips
16 ounces of unsalted, dry roasted peanuts

Combine the two packages of chips. Microwave on high for 2 ½ to 3 minutes or melt in a double boiler or in a small pan in a larger pan of water. Add peanuts. Microwave for another 2 minutes or 4 minutes in pan while stirring. Drop spoonfuls on an ungreased cookie sheet. Refrigerate for one hour.

BLACK BOTTOM CUPCAKES

8 ounces of cream cheese
½ cup of sugar
1 lightly beaten egg
6 ounces of chocolate chips
1 devil's food cake mix

Beat cream cheese, sugar and egg until creamy then fold in chocolate chips. Prepare cake mix as directed and fill cupcakes to one-third full. Add a heaping spoonful of the cream cheese mixture and cover with cake mix to two-thirds full. Bake at 350 degrees for 20 to 25 minutes.

BUCKEYES

1 package of graham crackers, crushed
2¾ cups of powdered sugar
1 cup of peanut butter (crunchy or smooth)
1 cup of butter, melted
Chocolate or chocolate chips, melted

Combine crumbs and sugar. Melt butter and peanut butter then add to crumb mixture. Form into balls about 1½ inches in diameter. Chill, dip into melted chocolate and chill again.

"DUMP IT IN" CAKE

20 ounces of crushed pineapple with juice
20 ounces of canned cherry pie filling
1 box of yellow cake mix
4 tablespoons of butter
½ cup of chopped nuts

Spread pineapple on the bottom of a 9-inch by 13-inch pan. Pour pie filling over the fruit and cover with the dry cake mix. Drizzle butter over everything and top with nuts. Do not stir or mix. Bake at 350 degrees for 1 hour.

FIVE-MINUTE KEY LIME PIE

1 prepared graham cracker piecrust
12 ounces of key lime yogurt
1 small package of lime gelatin
¼ cup of boiling water
8 ounces of whipped topping

In a large bowl, dissolve gelatin in boiling water. Stir in yogurt with a whisk. Fold in whipped topping. Spread into the piecrust and refrigerate overnight.

FRIDGE-BAKED CHOCOLATE PIE

20 Regular-sized marshmallows
2/3 cup of milk
1 8-inch graham cracker piecrust
4 small Hershey chocolate bars
1 cup whipped cream

Combine chocolate bars, milk and marshmallows in a double boiler or similar set-up until melted. Water should not be hot but not boiling. Let mixture cool then fold in whipped cream and pour into piecrust. Refrigerate.

FUDGESICLES

1 package of instant chocolate pudding
½ cup of cream
1/8 cup of sugar
Milk as directed on box

Mix well, preferably with a mixer. Pour into small paper cups and freeze. If you want to use sticks, cover cups with plastic wrap to hold stick in place.

GORP

Raisins
Dry roasted peanuts or almonds
Sunflower seeds, shelled
Rolled Oats
M&Ms, carob, chocolate or vanilla chips

Mix equal parts of each ingredient and store in a sealed container or Ziploc bag.

PEANUT BUTTER FUDGE

¼ cup of honey
½ cup of peanut butter
¾ cup of dry powdered milk

Mix ingredients together and smooth into an 8-inch by 8-inch pan. Chill four 3 hours in the refrigerator.

PEPPERMINT BARK

12 ounces of white chocolate chips/pieces
24 hard peppermint candies or
10 small candy canes

Line a baking sheet with wax paper. Put chocolate in a bowl and microwave on high for 1 minute then stir. Continue to microwave for 15 second intervals, stirring each time until chocolate is smooth. Place peppermint candy in a strong plastic bag and crush well. Sprinkle the small pieces into the chocolate and hold back the bigger chunks. Spread the mixture onto the wax paper to about ¼ inch in thickness. Top chocolate mixture with the larger peppermint pieces and let cool for 1 to 2 hours. Break into bark-sized chunks.

POTATO CHIP COOKIES

3½ cups of flour
1½ cups of brown sugar
1½ cups of crushed potato chips
1½ cups of chopped nuts
2 cups of shortening
1 teaspoon of vanilla

Mix shortening, sugar and vanilla together thoroughly. Add flour, potato chips and nuts. Drop spoonfuls on to a cookie sheet. Bake at 350 degrees for 10 to 12 minutes.

SUNDAY NIGHT COOKIES

¼ cup of brown sugar
½ cup of margarine (softened)
1 cup of flour
1 teaspoon of vanilla

Mix all ingredients and form into 1-inch balls then place on a cookie sheet. Bake at 350 degrees for 10 minutes.

TWINKIE CAKE

2 boxes of Twinkies
2 boxes of vanilla pudding
1 quart of strawberries
Cool Whip

Line a 9-inch by 12-inch glass dish with Twinkies. Mix pudding as directed on the box. Layer half the pudding over the Twinkies, followed by strawberries and then the rest of the pudding. Top with Cool Whip and refrigerate.

WHITE PRETZELS

12 ounces of white chocolate pieces
1 cup of pretzels sticks or 1-inch pieces
1 cup of dry roasted peanuts

Melt chocolate in a double boiler or in a small pan in a larger pan of water. Once melted add in the pretzel pieces and peanuts and stir. Drop spoonfuls onto wax paper. Refrigerate for 1 hour.

WORLD'S EASIEST COOKIE

Guys, even you can pull this one off. It's three ingredients, but don't burn the chips! Keep the heat low.

6 ounces of butterscotch chips
12 ounces of chocolate chips
1 large package of chow mien noodles

Melt chips together and then stir in noodles thoroughly. Drop cookies on wax paper with a spoon and let cool.

YOGURT GRANOLA SUNDAE

1 cup of vanilla yogurt
1 cup of granola mix
2 bananas, sliced
1 pint of blueberries or strawberries,
   washed and sliced

Layer yogurt, granola and fruit in parfait glasses or bowls. Refrigerate for 2 hours and serve.

DRINKS

BLACK COW

2 scoops of vanilla ice cream
12 ounces of root beer (1 can)
1 ounce of chocolate syrup
Whip cream

Scoop ice cream into a tall glass. Pour root beer over the ice cream, drizzle with chocolate sauce and top with whip cream.

CHRISTMAS BREAK COFFEE

1 cup of hot chocolate mix
1 cup of non-dairy creamer
½ cup instant coffee
½ teaspoon cinnamon
¼ teaspoon nutmeg
½ to ¾ cup sugar

Mix hot chocolate, creamer, coffee, cinnamon and nutmeg in a blender. Add in sugar and blend well. Drop in 3 to 4 heaping teaspoons per mug and pour in hot water.

CLOSED DANCE PUNCH

4 cups of grape juice
6 cups of orange juice
4 cups of lemon juice
3 cups of pineapple juice
10 cups of ginger ale
5 cups of sugar
5 cups of water

Combine all liquid ingredients. Mix in sugar until completely dissolved. Chill for 2 to 3 hours.

CRANBERRY LIME COOLER

6 ounces of frozen limeade concentrate, thawed
4 cups of cold water
2 cups of cranberry juice cocktail
2 cups of lemon-lime pop (Sprite, 7-Up, etc.)

Combine concentrate, water and cranberry juice. Mix well and refrigerate. When ready to serve add in the pop.

DO-IT-YOURSELF ROOT BEER

2 cups sugar
½ bottle root beer extract
1 teaspoon of dry yeast
½ cup warm water
1 to 2 cups water

Pour 3 tablespoons or ½ bottle of root beer extract over 2 cups sugar and add enough water to dissolve. Add 1 teaspoon dry yeast to ½ cup warm water to dissolve. Add both mixtures together and pour into gallon jug. Top of jug with warm water and let set for 6 hours uncapped. Tighten lid and refrigerate. After 24 hours it's ready to drink. The longer it sets, the better it tastes.

FRESH SQUEEZED LEMONADE

6 cups of water
¾ cup of sugar
1 tablespoon of grated lemon peel
½ cup of fresh lemon juice

In a pitcher dissolve sugar in water. Stir in peel and juice. Refrigerate for at least 2 hours.

HOMECOMING PUNCH

12 ounces of frozen concentrated
    white grape juice
3 pints of pineapple juice
24 ounces of lemon-lime soda

Mix grape juice according to directions. Combine grape juice with pineapple juice and lemon-lime soda. Mix thoroughly.

ICED CAPPUCCINO

1½ cups of strong coffee
½ cup of sweetened condensed milk
½ cup of half-and-half
½ teaspoon of vanilla
Ice

Combine coffee and milk. Whisk in half-and-half and vanilla until they are well blended. Pour into ice-filled glass.

JULIUS OF ORANGE

3 ounces of frozen orange juice concentrate
½ cup of milk
½ cup of water
¼ cup of sugar
½ teaspoon of vanilla
6 ice cubes

Put all ingredients in a blender. Blend until smooth, about 30 to 40 seconds.

PINK LEMONADE MILKSHAKE

3 cups milk
10 scoops vanilla ice cream
1½ cups of frozen pink lemonade
        concentrate

Mix together in a blender. Works with regular lemonade too.

PROTEIN SHAKE

2 cups of milk
¾ cup of ice cream
2 raw eggs
Vanilla to taste
Sugar to taste

Put ingredients into a blender and mix on high until it achieves milkshake consistency.

VIRGIN DAIQUIRI

1 ounce of lime juice
3 ounces of strawberries
1 tablespoon of sugar
Crushed ice

Put ice in a blender, followed by lime juice, sugar and strawberries. Blend until smooth then pour into a chilled glass.

For information on the entire series of Tim Murphy's "Cookbooks for Guys" and his other books visit www.flanneljohn.com.

Made in the USA
San Bernardino, CA
09 July 2015